KETO PIZZA & PASTA COOKBOOK

*Quick, Easy and Delicious Low-Carb
Ketogenic Italian Recipes to Enhance
Weight Loss and Healthy Living*

TABLE OF CONTENTS

INTRODUCTION

Going keto has become THE diet fad to beat these days.

The keto diet has captured the attention of people the way no other diet was able to in the last decade or so. In fact, Google gets no fewer than a million searches every month about this particular diet.

Taking research, testimonials, survey results, and other similar factors into consideration, it does not seem surprising at all that more and more people are jumping on the keto bandwagon.

An incredible number of people attribute the success of their weight loss efforts to the keto diet. Moreover, going on a keto diet seems to do more than just help you lose weight. It apparently also helps to make your heart stronger, to increase your energy levels, and improve brain function and memory. In short, it enhances your health and wellbeing.

This book provides recipes that are in line with the ketogenic diet. However, it does more than this. It includes only recipes that are Italian in inspiration.

Italian cuisine has long held its position as one of the world's leading cooking styles. Known for its abundance of flavors, as well as its simplicity in preparation, Italian food continues to influence a great number of cuisines around the globe. No one can deny its tremendous popularity – not when people across the world now think of pizza and pasta as part of their own national cuisines.

This book provides no less than 60 mouth-watering Italian recipes that range from antipasti, entrees, to desserts. It tweaks recipes so that you are able to enjoy the taste and flavors of Italian home-cooking AND still remain faithful to a healthy keto diet.

Just because you are on a diet does not mean that you have to go without your favorite Italian dishes. This book ensures that you enjoy the best of both worlds.

Thanks for purchasing this book, I hope you enjoy it!

CHAPTER 1

THE KETO DIET AND HOW IT PROMOTES WEIGHT LOSS AND HEALTHY LIVING

What is keto diet? How did it become so popular in so short a time?

A keto eating plan centers on foods rich in healthy fats. It includes a moderate amount of protein-rich foods, and limits intake of carbohydrates. When you embrace a keto diet, your primary goal is to get most of your calories from healthy fat, rather than from carbs.

The body uses glucose as its main source of fuel or energy. For most people, this means eating foods rich in sugar and refined carbohydrates. When you go on a ketogenic diet, however, you exclude these foods from your diet as much as you can.

What happens when you go keto?

Your body runs short of glucose to use as energy. Constrained to look for other means to support its energy requirements, it starts to break down fats.

Using fat for energy is a metabolic process called ketosis. When the body fails to access glucose for energy, it transforms fat into a type of acid called ketones which tissues and muscles use for fuel.

An increasing number of people are using ketosis as an effective means to lose weight and promote healthy living. By going on a keto diet, they find that they are able to burn more calories, lose weight, reduce body fat – and become healthier, in the process.

Going on a keto diet triggers certain changes in your body that are linked to many health benefits.

- You burn more fat.

When you go on a keto diet, you force your body to use fat instead of carbs as your primary source of energy. When you burn fat, you use up more calories – and lose weight.

- You enjoy a quicker and healthier metabolism.

A keto diet makes way for faster metabolism.

Studies suggest that when your body runs on fat, it produces more heat. This helps to speed up metabolism – and facilitates losing weight.

- You don't get hungry as often.

A keto diet makes you stay off foods with high glycemic index – foods that promote sugar spikes that are immediately followed by a crash in energy.

The glycemic index (GI) indicates how quickly the body converts the carbs contained in a particular food into glucose.

Foods with high GI values convert into glucose faster. White bread and refined sugars belong to this category. They are easily digested and are quickly converted into glucose which your body burns quickly. As a result, you tend to feel hungry sooner even if you have just eaten.

Foods with low GI values are more slowly digested. Whole grains, leafy vegetables, lean meat, and fatty fish belong to this category. Filling up on such foods helps you to feel full for a longer period of time. It takes the edge off your appetite, staves off hunger, and helps you manage your food cravings.

- Your body gets the nutrients that it needs.

Foods high in carbs go through processes that strip them of most of their fiber and nutrients. Although usually high in calories, they fail to provide your body with the nutrition that it requires.

A keto diet includes omega 3 fatty acid-rich fish like salmon, mackerel, sardines, shrimp, and oysters. It includes healthy seeds and nuts like chia seeds, walnuts, soybeans, and almonds. It includes vegetables like cauliflower, zucchini, bell peppers, asparagus, spinach and other non-starchy vegetables and leafy greens. It includes healthy oils like olive oil, coconut oil, and avocado oil.

These foods not only provide steady and sustained energy; they also give you the nutrients that you need to live a healthy life.

- Your blood sugar stays within manageable levels.

A low-carb keto diet prevents diabetes. It helps you lower your blood sugar. Studies show that people who already have type-2 diabetes are even able to reduce their insulin dosage when they go on low-carb, keto diets.

- It makes the heart stronger.

A diet centered on healthy fat – avocados, fatty fish, olive oil, cheese – helps to increase the 'good' cholesterol high density lipoprotein and reduce the 'bad' cholesterol low-density lipoprotein. As a result, the diet helps you fight plaque build-up and avoid heart disease and stroke.

- It makes your brain function more effectively.

Your brain needs the right foods to keep it at peak condition. Foods rich in antioxidants, omega 3 fatty acids, and other brain-friendly nutrients keep the brain sharp and efficient.

It makes for a long, healthy life.

A low-carb keto diet helps nourish the body. It protects you from the ill effects of inflammation and oxidative stress. As a result, you have more energy and stamina. You avoid getting sick. You look and feel young. You are able to stay healthy and productive for a longer time.

CHAPTER 2

LIST OF MUST-HAVE INGREDIENTS

Preparing low-carb and keto-friendly recipes is not only healthy. It is also easy, convenient, and fun, especially if you have the right ingredients in your pantry.

What are the ingredients that you should keep in stock if you intend to stay on a healthy keto diet?

- Fish and seafood

Salmon, mackerel, sardines, oysters, mussels, clams, shrimp and other seafood are keto-friendly ingredients.

Fatty fish are rich in omega 3 fatty acids while shellfish is rich in selenium, potassium, and B vitamins. Both are practically carbs-free.

- Vegetables

Vegetables are ideal for keto diets. They are low in carbs and calories, high in fiber, and rich in vitamins, antioxidants, minerals, and other nutrients. They are not only nutritious; they are also very versatile ingredients.

Bell peppers, tomatoes, eggplant, olives, cauliflower, broccoli, kale, green beans, artichokes, spinach and other leafy greens are great go-to vegetables for keto recipes.

You can use spaghetti squash to take the place of spaghetti and zucchini to create zucchini noodles or "zoodles" for your pasta recipes. Cauliflower is also popular as a low-carb substitute for mashed potatoes or rice. Onions and garlic add great flavor (and nutrients) to recipes.

- Poultry and meat

Beef, pork, and chicken hardly have any carbs. They are rich sources of minerals like zinc, selenium, and potassium, as well as of high-quality protein and B vitamins.

- Eggs

Eggs are nutritious and versatile. They help to stabilize blood sugar levels and promote satiety, leading to lower food intake.

- Berries

A good number of fruits have too much sugar, making them unsuitable for the low-carb keto diet. Berries like blackberries, raspberries, blueberries, strawberries are an exception. They do not have as much sugar as other fruits. They are also loaded with fiber, as well antioxidants that protect the body against diseases.

- Avocado

Avocado is also well suited to a keto diet. It is high in good fats, vitamins, and minerals, especially potassium.

- Seeds and nuts

Roasted nuts and seeds make for healthy low-carb/high-fat tasty snacks. They are also great as add-ons to entrees, appetizers, and desserts for their crunch and great nutty flavor.

See to it that you have some of these nuts and seeds in your pantry: almonds, cashews, pecans, walnuts, pumpkin seeds, flaxseeds, sesame seeds, and chia seeds.

- Shirataki noodles

Shirataki noodles are an amazing addition to any pantry. Available in shapes like linguine, fettuccine, and rice, they can be used in place of regular noodles and are fantastic for Italian pasta recipes.

With its high water content and low-carb content, Shirataki noodles help control hunger and facilitate digestion.

- Cheese

Cheese is rich, delicious, and nourishing. It adds great texture and flavor to any recipe.

There are many types of cheese. Most of them are low-carb, as well as rich in calcium, protein, and beneficial fatty acids, making them an amazing fit for a keto-friendly diet.

You may want to stock up on the following cheeses – mozzarella, ricotta, cheddar, parmesan, Asiago, and Parmigiano-Reggiano

- Olive oil

Olive oil is a pure no-carb fat source that is extremely heart-friendly.

It has oleic acid, a naturally occurring fatty acid that helps to reduce risk factors associated with heart disease.

It is also rich in antioxidants that strengthen the arteries, decrease inflammation, and protect the heart.

It can be used to sauté food in or to make salad dressing when combined with balsamic vinegar or fruit acids.

- Coconut oil

Coconut oil has unique properties that render it suitable for a keto diet.

The MCTs (medium-chain triglycerides) in coconut oil help you quickly convert the oil into ketones that the body can use immediately for fuel.

Studies also show that the intake of coconut oil helps people shed fat, particularly in the belly region, and lose weight.

- Cocoa powder and dark chocolate

Cocoa powder and dark chocolate are not only ingredients that make dessert recipes delicious. Produced from cacao, both substances are rich in antioxidants that lower blood pressure and keep the heart healthy.

- Sugar-free sweeteners

Ketosis requires you to reduce or totally eliminate sugar from your diet. Fortunately, you can use sugar-free sweeteners to sweeten your dressings, sauces, desserts, and baked goods.

The following are popular sugar-free sweeteners you can use:

Stevia – a derivative from the plant called Stevia rebaudiana, stevia is a natural sweetener with practically no carbs or calories.

Erythritol is a sugar alcohol. It is almost as sweet as regular sugar but contains only 5% of its calories.

CHAPTER 3

10 KETO ANTIPASTI/SIDE DISH RECIPES

1. CHEESE-STUFFED MUSHROOMS

Serves 4

Nutrition per serving:
432 calories

23 g Protein | 9 g Carbohydrates | 37 g Fat

Total Time: 35 minutes
Prep: 15 minutes
Cook: 20 minutes

INGREDIENTS:

- Portobello mushrooms, gills removed, 8 pieces
- Butter, melted, 2 tbsp
- Frozen spinach, drained, squeezed, chopped, 1 10 oz-pack
- Half of a red onion, minced
- Garlic, minced, ½ tsp
- Parmesan cheese, grated, ½ cup
- Cream cheese, 1 cup
- Ricotta cheese, ¼ cup
- Goat cheese, 3 ½ oz
- Cheddar cheese, grated, ¼ cup
- Red bell pepper, diced, 2 tbsp
- Dried Italian herbs, 1/8 tsp

PROCEDURE:

1. Pre-heat your oven to 400°F.
2. Dry the mushrooms by patting gently with paper towels.

3. Coat the mushrooms with the melted butter using a pastry brush. Arrange the mushrooms on a baking tray lined with parchment paper.
4. Combine the onion, garlic, spinach, goat cheese, cream cheese, ricotta, and Parmesan cheese in a bowl. Mix gently but thoroughly.
5. Spoon the cheese mixture generously onto the mushrooms.
6. Sprinkle the diced red pepper and the cheddar cheese on top of the cheese mixture.
7. Bake until the cheese mixture is bubbly – around 20 minutes.
8. Serve garnished with Italian herbs of choice.

2. OVEN-BAKED FRUITY-NUTTY GOAT CHEESE

Serves 4

Nutrition per serving:
584 calories

33 g Protein | 4 g Carbohydrates | 46 g Fat

Total Time: 25 minutes
Prep: 10 minutes
Cook: 15 minutes

INGREDIENTS:

- Goat cheese (or Brie or Camembert), 20 oz
- Pistachio nuts, roughly chopped, 1 oz

- Salt
- Rosemary (fresh)

Fruity sauce:

- Fresh blackberries (or raspberries), 9 oz

- Erythritol, 1 tbsp (optional)
- Ground cinnamon, a pinch

PROCEDURE:

1. Pre-heat your oven to 350°F.
2. Make the blackberry sauce by combining blackberries, sweetener (if desired), and ground cinnamon. Set aside.
3. Bake the goat cheese for 10-12 minutes or until it changes color. Take it out of the oven and let sit for about 5 minutes.
4. Roast the pistachios in an ungreased frying pan. Sprinkle with salt to taste.
5. Assemble your goat cheese platter. Spread the blackberry sauce on top of the goat cheese. Top with the roasted pistachios. Garnish with rosemary.

3. PROSCIUTTO AND CHICKEN SPIEDINI

Serves 8

Nutrition per serving:
174 calories

$\qquad$ *20 g Protein | 1 g Carbohydrates | 10 g Fat*

Total Time: 25 minutes
  Prep: 10 minutes
  Cook: 15 minutes

INGREDIENTS:

- Chicken tenders, 8 pieces
- Prosciutto, 8 pieces
- Salt, ½ tsp (seasoning)
- Black pepper, ground, 1/8 tsp (seasoning)
- Garlic powder, ¼ tsp (seasoning)
- Provolone cheese (or other cheeses), 8-oz block
- Basil leaves (fresh)
- 8 skewers

PROCEDURE:

1. Make the spice mixture by combining the seasoning ingredients in a small bowl.
2. Remove tendons from the chicken tenders. Pound or flatten them into thin, flat, even pieces.
3. Gently rub the chicken with the spice mixture to season.
4. Cut the cheese into 1x2 inch-pieces.
5. On a cutting board, lay a slice of prosciutto. Put a chicken tender on top. Put 1-2 basil leaves on top of the chicken tender. Put a piece of the Provolone cheese across the basil leaves, leaving space of about an inch on the edge facing you.
6. Roll the bundle with care. Put a skewer to hold the ingredients in place.
7. Repeat the process with the rest of the ingredients.
8. Grill the spiedini for 3 minutes on each side or until cooked through.
9. Serve warm.

4. EGGPLANT-CHEESE MELTS

Serves 2

Nutrition per serving:
277 calories

14 g Protein | 15 g Carbohydrates | 18 g Fat

Total Time: 13 minutes
   Prep: 3 minutes
   Cook: 10 minutes

INGREDIENTS:

- Eggplant, sliced into 6 pieces, 1
- Cooking spray
- Canned tomato sauce, 2 tbsp
- Basil leaves (fresh), shredded, 6 leaves
- Prosciutto, 6 slices
- Cheese, grated, 6 tbsp
- Black pepper to taste

PROCEDURE:

1. Pre-heat the overhead grill or broiler.
2. Put the eggplant slices on a paper-lined baking sheet. Spray with cooking oil.
3. Broil for 3 minutes. Flip the eggplant and broil the other side for about the same time.
4. Take the baking tray out of the grill and assemble the eggplant. Spread some tomato sauce on each eggplant slice. Add the basil leaves. Top with prosciutto. Sprinkle with cheese.
5. Return the tray to the grill and cook for a couple of minutes or until the cheese melts.
6. Before serving, season the eggplant-cheese melts with some freshly ground pepper.

5. SUB ROLL UPS

Serves 6

Nutrition per serving:
201 calories

14 g Protein | 2 g Carbohydrates | 15 g Fat

Total Time: 10 minutes
  Prep: 10 minutes

INGREDIENTS:

Roll ups:

- Pepperoni, 12 slices
- Ham, 6 slices
- Provolone cheese, 6 slices
- Lettuce, shredded, 2 cups
- Hot cherry peppers (canned), ¼ cup
- ¼ of a white onion, sliced thinly

Sauce:

- Mayonnaise (sugar-free), 2 tbsp
- Red wine vinegar, 1 tbsp
- Italian seasoning, 2 tsp

PROCEDURE:

1. Mix all the ingredients for the sauce in a small bowl.
2. Assemble the roll up layers – ham, cheese, pepperoni (2 slices), sauce, lettuce, peppers, and onion.
3. Roll up each piece carefully. Serve.

6. OLIVES & HERB FOCACCIA

Serves 6

Nutrition per serving:
144 calories

7 g Protein | 5 g Carbohydrates | 11 g Fat

Total Time: 25 minutes
  Prep: 10 minutes
  Cook: 15 minutes

INGREDIENTS:

Focaccia:

- Eggs, 4
- Yogurt (whole milk, plain) 2 heaping tbsp
- Coconut flour, 1/3 cup plus 1 tbsp
- Psyllium husks (whole), 2 ½ tbsp
- Salt, ½ tsp
- Baking powder (gluten-free), 1 tsp

Toppings:

- Kalamata olives, sliced, ¼ cup
- Herbs of choice (thyme, sage, and/ or rosemary), minced, 2 tbsp
- Olive oil (extra virgin), 2 tbsp
- Salt, pinch

PROCEDURE:

1. Pre-heat your oven to 375°F.
2. Whisk the eggs in a large bowl. Add the yogurt and continue whisking.
3. Add all the dry ingredients for the foccacia and stir until you get thick dough that forms into a ball.
4. Put the dough on a paper-lined baking tray and shape it into a 1/2"-thick rectangle. Set aside.
5. Heat the olive oil, herbs, and salt in a small pot over low heat until the herbs release their fragrance.

6. Put the sliced olives on top of the focaccia. Drizzle with the seasoned olive oil.
7. Put the dough in the oven to bake for about 15 minutes.

7. ANTIPASTO SALAD

Serves 8

Nutrition per serving:
345 calories

14 g Protein | 3 g Carbohydrates | 30 g Fat

Total Time: 10 minutes
   Prep: 10 minutes

INGREDIENTS:

- White wine vinegar, 1 tbsp
- Olive oil, 3 tbsp
- Black pepper, ¼ tsp
- Salt, ¼ tsp
- Kalamata olives, ½ cup
- Fresh mozzarella balls
- Pepperoncini peppers, drained and chopped, 1 cup
- Artichoke hearts, drained and chopped, 1 can (14-oz)
- Grape tomatoes, halved, 2 cups
- Prosciutto, chopped, 6 oz
- Salami, chopped, 8 oz
- Basil (fresh), sliced into ribbons, ¼ cup

PROCEDURE:

1. Whisk to combine wine vinegar, olive oil, black pepper, and salt.
2. Toss all the other ingredients, except for the basil, in the dressing.
3. Garnish with basil.

8. CHEESE CRISPS

Serves 4

Nutrition per serving:
92 calories

7 g Protein | 1 g Carbohydrates | 7 g Fat

Total Time: 13 minutes
  Prep: 5 minutes
  Cook: 8 minutes

INGREDIENTS:

- Italian blend cheese, shredded, 1 cup
- Italian seasoning, 2 tsp

PROCEDURE:

1. Pre-heat your oven to 350°F.
2. Prepare 2 parchment paper-lined baking trays.
3. Use a measuring spoon (1 tablespoon) to drop the shredded cheese in small heaps on the tray. See to it that you keep a space of 2 inches in between each heap as the cheese is going to spread while baking.
4. Top each heap with a pinch of the seasoning.
5. Bake the cheese crisps for 5 to 8 minutes. Check them so they don't burn.
6. Put the crisps on racks to cool. Pat off excess grease with a paper towel.

9. STUFFED ARTICHOKES

Serves 4

Nutrition per serving:
420 calories

14 g Protein | 21 g Carbohydrates | 33 g Fat

Total Time: 1 hr, 15 minutes
    Prep: 20 minutes
    Cook: 55 minutes

INGREDIENTS:

Artichokes:

- Globe artichokes, 4
- Lemon juice, 1 tsp
- Water, ¾ cup

Stuffing:

- Almond flour (blanched, superfine) 1 cup
- Asiago cheese, grated, ½ cup
- Butter, melted, 6 tbsp
- Lemon zest, 1 tsp
- Red bell pepper, minced, 1 tbsp
- Dried onion flakes, 1 tsp
- Garlic, minced, 1 tsp
- Parsley, chopped, 1 tbsp
- Ground black pepper, ¼ tsp
- Salt, 1 tsp

PROCEDURE:

1. Combine all the ingredients for the stuffing, stirring well. Set aside.
2. Using a serrated knife, remove 2 inches off of the top of the artichokes. Remove the bottom stems as well to make the artichokes stay upright.
3. Rinse the artichokes under running water. Cook the artichokes, uncovered, in the microwave on high for about 3-5 minutes. Set aside to cool
4. In the meantime, pre-heat your oven to 375°F.
5. When the artichokes are cool enough, remove the center leaves. Use a spoon to scoop out the stubbly "choke" found in the center.

6. Using your fingers, rub the center with lemon juice to prevent browning.
7. Use ¼ of the stuffing to stuff the center of each artichoke. Put some stuffing between the leaves, as well.
8. Put the artichokes in a baking dish. Cover with foil.
9. Bake the artichokes for about 40 to 50 minutes or until cooked through. Take the foil off and cook for another 3-5 minutes.
10. Serve hot.

10. MUSHROOMS IN OLIVE OIL AND GARLIC BUTTER

Serves 4

Nutrition per serving:
141 calories

4 g Protein | 4 g Carbohydrates | 13 g Fat

Total Time: 25 minutes
  Prep: 5 minutes
  Cook: 20 minutes

INGREDIENTS:

- Mushrooms (Cremini or Portobello), rinsed, patted dry with paper towels, sliced, 1 lb
- Olive oil, 2 tbsp (divided)
- Salt, ½ tsp
- Black pepper, ¼ tsp
- Butter, 2 tbsp
- Garlic, minced, 2 cloves
- Chicken broth, ¼ cup

PROCEDURE:

1. Heat half of the olive oil in a skillet for about 2 minutes.
2. Add half of the mushrooms to sauté. Flip them halfway through. Cook for 4 to 5 minutes until the mushrooms turn light brown in color and reduce in size as the liquid evaporates. Stir in salt and pepper to taste. Set the cooked mushrooms aside.
3. Add the remaining olive oil and sauté the last half of the mushrooms the same way.
4. Add the butter to the skillet. Once it melts, add the minced garlic and cook until fragrant (about 1 or 2 minutes). Add the rest of the cooked mushrooms. Cook for a couple of minutes so the mushrooms absorb the flavors.
5. Add the broth and gently scrape the bottom of the skillet with a wooden spoon.
6. Bring the broth to a simmer and cook for an additional 2 or 3 minutes.

CHAPTER 4

20 KETO PASTA RECIPES

Pasta being one of the more popular ingredients in Italian cuisine, a traditional Italian kitchen will have a wide variety of pasta in its pantry. Grain-based pasta, however, has high carbohydrate content. It is a no-no in a keto diet.

Fortunately, you CAN enjoy delicious Italian pasta recipes and still remain faithful to your keto diet. Simply substitute your regular pasta with zucchini noodles or Shirataki noodles.

Zucchini Noodles

Zoodles is a term for noodles or pasta made from zucchini. It has become very popular over the last ten years, especially with the rising interest in going keto.

Like regular pasta, zucchini noodles are neutral in flavor; they easily absorb flavors in pasta sauces. They are also inexpensive and easy to spiralize or form into pasta shape.

Use the following steps and tips for preparing pasta recipes that call for zucchini noodles.

Get the zucchini and cut off both ends.

Insert the zucchini securely in your vegetable spiralizer and give it a twist to get your spiral of noodles.

As an alternative, use a mandoline or a vegetable peeler to form strands that look like wide tagliatelle pasta.

You can also use a julienne slicer to give your zucchini noodles a shape very similar to that of spaghetti.

Whatever kitchen gadget you decide to use, see to it that you do not include the seedy portion of the zucchini.

Pasta is best when cooked al dente. Zucchini has a lot of water. Your zucchini noodles may turn soggy or mushy if you overcook them even by just a couple of minutes.

Most people prefer to just heat zucchini noodles up instead of cooking them. This means using them raw and crisp and simply allowing the heat from pasta sauce to warm them up.

If you don't want to eat them raw, cook them in the microwave for a minute. If you are cooking the noodles in large amounts, microwave them in 30-second increments so you can easily check for doneness.

If you are using the stovetop to prepare your pasta sauce, you can also sauté your noodles. Put a little olive oil in a pan and sauté the noodles for a minute or two.

Shirataki Pasta

Shirataki are traditional Japanese noodles. They are bland, low calorie, low carb noodles that make use of konjac yam. They are gelatinous and translucent, their appearance conjuring up visions of a white waterfall or "shirataki" in Japanese.

Shirataki noodles have found their way into Italian pasta dishes. The noodles have no particular flavor on their own which make them perfect for absorbing the flavors of Italian pasta sauces.

For recipes that use Shirataki noodles, prepare pasta in the following manner:

Rinse the noodles. Put in a pot of boiling water and cook for 2 minutes. Drain.

Dry roast the noodles by putting them in a skillet and roasting them over medium heat for a minute.

PASTA RECIPES

1. SHRIMP IN VELVETY GARLIC SAUCE

Serves 4

Nutrition per serving:
508 calories

31 g Protein | 8 g Carbohydrates | 44 g Fat

Total Time: 20 minutes
  Prep: 10 minutes
  Cook: 10 minutes

INGREDIENTS:

- Olive oil, 1 tbsp
- Shrimp, deveined, 1 lb
- Salt
- Pepper
- Butter, 2 tbsp
- Garlic, minced, 6 cloves
- Dry white wine, ½ cup
- Cream (reduced fat), 1 ½ cups
- Parmesan cheese grated, ½ cup
- Zucchini noodles, 4 cups
- Parsley, chopped, 2 tbsp

PROCEDURE:

1. Heat the olive oil in a skillet.
2. Cook the shrimps for a couple of minutes, seasoning them midway with salt and pepper. Flip the shrimps to cook the other side. Transfer the cooked shrimps to a bowl. Set aside.
3. Using the same skillet, melt the butter. Cook the garlic in the butter for about 30 seconds. Add the wine, gently scrape the browned bits off the bottom of the skillet, and continue cooking until the wine reduces to half its original amount.
4. Add the cream to the skillet and gently simmer. Season the sauce with salt and pepper.
5. Add the cheese to thicken the sauce, cooking for 1 -2 minutes.
6. Add the cooked shrimps to the skillet. Adjust seasonings.
7. Add the zucchini noodles and toss to coat with sauce.
8. Garnish with parsley.

2. ZOODLES WITH ALFREDO SAUCE

Serves 8

Nutrition per serving:
249 calories

4 g Protein | 6 g Carbohydrates | 23 g Fat

Time: 30 minutes
Prep: 10 minutes
Cook: 20 minutes

INGREDIENTS:

- Zucchini noodles, 4 cups
- Butter, 2 tbsp
- Garlic, crushed, 2 cloves
- Cream cheese, 2 oz
- Heavy cream, 1 ½ cups
- Parmesan cheese, grated, ½ cup
- White ground pepper, ½ tsp
- Ground nutmeg, ¼ tsp
- Salt

PROCEDURE:

1. Melt the butter in a saucepan. Add the garlic and cook until fragrant or for about 2 minutes.
2. Add the cream cheese to melt. Add the heavy cream and simmer slowly.
3. Gradually add the Parmesan cheese while whisking the cream.
4. Simmer for 8-10 minutes. Season the sauce with salt, pepper and nutmeg.
5. Serve the sauce over zucchini noodles.

3. GNOCCHI IN SEASONED BUTTER

Serves 4

Nutrition per serving:
414 calories

20 g Protein | 5 g Carbohydrates | 35 g Fat

Total Time: 25 minutes
  Prep: 20 minutes (plus 1 hr and 15 minutes inactive time)
  Cook: 5 minutes

INGREDIENTS:

Pasta:

- Almond flour, 1 ½ cups
- Coconut flour, 1 tbsp
- Xanthan gum, 2 tsp
- Ricotta cheese, grated, ½ lb
- Parmesan cheese, grated, ½ cup
- Egg, lightly beaten, 1
- Salt
- Pepper

Seasoned butter:

- Butter, 4 tbsp
- Olive oil, 1 tbsp
- Sage, 8 leaves
- Garlic, finely sliced, 2 cloves

PROCEDURE:

1. Put the flours and xanthan gum in a mixing bowl and stir to combine.
2. In another bowl, mix the cheeses until thoroughly combined.
3. Add the flour mixture, salt, pepper and egg to the cheeses. Stir until you get smooth and somewhat sticky dough.
4. Wrap the dough in plastic wrap and refrigerate for an hour.
5. After an hour, take the dough out of the refrigerator. Form into balls around an inch in diameter.
6. Line a baking sheet with parchment paper. Put the balls on the sheet and press down lightly to form the gnocchi.
7. Put the gnocchi in the freezer for 15 minutes.

8. To cook the gnocchi, get a skillet and gently heat the olive oil and butter.
9. Add the sliced garlic and sage. Add the gnocchi and cook for about 5 minutes, gently stirring once in a while to prevent it from sticking to the pan.
10. Serve the pasta warm.

4. ROASTED CAULIFLOWER ZITI

Serves 6

Nutrition per serving:
536 calories

44 g Protein | 20 g Carbohydrates | 30 g Fat

Total Time: 1 hr, 10 minutes
  Prep: 15 minutes
  Cook: 55 minutes

INGREDIENTS:

Cauliflower Ziti:

- Cauliflower, cut into florets, 2 heads
- Olive oil, 2 tbsp
- Salt

Sauce:

- Olive oil (extra virgin), 1 tbsp
- Onion, chopped, 1
- Garlic, minced, 2 cloves
- Red pepper flakes, pinch
- Ground beef, 1 lb
- Salt
- Black pepper, (freshly ground)
- Tomato paste, 2 tbsp
- Dried oregano, 1 tsp
- Crushed tomatoes, 1 28 oz-can
- Basil, sliced thinly, 2 tbsp (add more for garnish if desired)
- Ricotta cheese (fresh), 1 ½ cups
- Mozzarella cheese, shredded, 2 cups
- Parmesan cheese, grated, ½ cup

PROCEDURE:

1. Pre-heat your oven to 375°F.
2. Make the cauliflower "ziti."
   Toss the cauliflower florets in olive oil and salt.
   Spread the florets evenly between 2 baking sheets and roast for 40 minutes or until the florets are tender and a light golden color. Set aside.

3. Make the sauce.

   In a large saucepan, heat the olive oil.

   Add the onions and sauté for 5 minutes.

   Add the garlic and red pepper flakes and sauté for another minute.

   Add the ground meat. Season with salt and pepper according to taste and cook for about 6-8 minutes or until the meat is no longer pink. Drain off the excess oil or fat.

   Add the tomato sauce. Season with dried oregano and cook for about 2 minutes or until the sauce turns a slightly darker red.

   Put in the crushed tomatoes and cook for an additional 10-15 minutes, stirring occasionally.

   Take the saucepan off the heat and add the basil. Combine the sauce and the cauliflower florets.

4. Assemble the pasta.

   Get a baking dish and put half of the cauliflower mixture. Spread gently and evenly. Top with half of the ricotta, mozzarella, and Parmesan cheese.

   Add another layer of the cauliflower and top with the remaining half of the cheeses.

5. Bake the "ziti" for 25-30 minutes or until the cheese melts and turns golden.

6. Garnish with basil if using.

5. ZUCCHINI RIBBONS IN WALNUT-AVOCADO PESTO

Serves 2

Nutrition per serving:
325 calories

> *11 g Protein | 11 g Carbohydrates | 26 g Fat*

Total Time: 15 minutes
  Prep: 10 minutes
  Cook: 5 minutes

INGREDIENTS:

- Zucchini noodles, 2 cups

Pesto sauce:

- Half an avocado
- Basil leaves (fresh), 1 cup
- Walnuts, ¼ cup
- Garlic, minced, 2 cloves
- Juice of half a lemon
- Parmesan cheese, grated, ¼ cup
- Water, as needed, about ½ cup
- Salt
- Pepper
- Italian seasoning, dash (optional)

Garnish (optional):

- Parmesan cheese
- Basil, 5 leaves

PROCEDURE:

1. Make the walnut-avocado pesto by putting all the ingredients for the pesto sauce in a blender. Blend until you get a smooth consistency, adding water as needed if the sauce is too thick.
2. Arrange the zucchini noodles in two bowls. Ladle the walnut-avocado pesto sauce over the zucchini noodles and toss very gently to coat.
3. Garnish with grated Parmesan cheese and basil leaves, if desired.

6. BACON ALFREDO IN EGGPLANT PASTA

Serves 6

Nutrition per serving:
564 calories

>*17 g Protein | 6 g Carbohydrates | 51 g Fat*

Total Time: 30 minutes
*   Prep: 10 minutes*
*   Cook: 20 minutes*

INGREDIENTS:

- Bacon, chopped, 1 lb
- Eggplant, peeled and julienned, 1 ½ lb
- Whipping cream, 1 cup
- Butter, 2 tbsp
- Garlic, grated, 2 cloves
- White wine, 1 tbsp
- Lemon juice, 1 tbsp
- Parmesan cheese, grated, 1 cup
- Basil leaves, for garnish (optional)

PROCEDURE:

1. Fry the bacon in a large skillet until it renders its fat and becomes crisp (about 10-15 minutes).
2. Drain the bacon on paper towels.
3. Cook the julienned eggplant "pasta" in bacon grease in the same skillet until it soaks up all the grease.
4. Make a well in the middle of the pasta and add the butter. Stir the eggplant noodles to coat with the melted butter.
5. Add the grated garlic. Cook for 2 minutes.
6. Add the whipping cream, wine, and lemon juice. Stir to combine so that the eggplant pasta absorbs all the flavors.
7. Add the cheese and half of the cooked bacon. Stir to combine.
8. Top with the remaining bacon.
9. Garnish with basil leaves, if using.

7. MEATBALLS ON VEGGIE NOODLES

Serves 2

Nutrition per serving:
446 calories

27 g Protein | 23 g Carbohydrates | 24 g Fat

Total Time: 35 minutes
  Prep: 5 minutes
  Cook: 30 minutes

INGREDIENTS:

Meatballs:

- Ground beef, 6 oz
- Rosemary, chopped finely, 1 tbsp
- Thyme, chopped finely, ½ tbsp

Pasta:

- Zucchini, spiralized, 2
- Sweet potato, spiralized, 1
- Carrots, spiralized, 2

- Avocado oil, 1 tbsp
- Salt
- Pepper
- Green olives, 10-15 pieces

PROCEDURE:

1. Preheat oven to 350°F. Line a baking sheet with parchment paper. Brush with a thin layer of avocado oil to keep the meatballs from sticking to the sheet. Set the sheet aside.
2. Prepare the meatballs.
   Combine the ground beef with the herbs. Mix well.
   Wet your hands. Pick up a scoop of the seasoned ground beef and

form into a ball about an inch in diameter. Do the same with the rest of the ground meat.

Put the meatballs on the baking sheet and bake for about 20 minutes.

3. In the meantime, heat the avocado oil in a wide saucepan, swirling it around so that it coats the entire pan.

4. Sauté the zucchini, sweet potato, and carrots in the avocado oil until the "pasta" wilts (about 5 minutes). Keep the pasta warm on low heat.

5. When the meatballs are ready, divide the pasta into 2 plates. Top with the meatballs. Season with salt and pepper to taste and garnish with olives.

8. CREAMY SALMON IN ZUCCHINI NOODLES

Serves 2

Nutrition per serving:
470 calories

> *21 g Protein | 4 g Carbohydrates | 42 g Fat*

Total Time: 10 minutes
Prep: 5 minutes
Cook: 5 minutes

INGREDIENTS:

- Coconut oil, 2 tbsp
- Smoked salmon, diced, 8 oz
- Zucchini, spiralized, 2 cups
- Mayonnaise, ¼ cup

PROCEDURE:

1. Heat the oil. Sauté the salmon for 2-3 minutes or until it turns slightly brown. Set the salmon aside.
2. Using the same pan, add the zucchini noodles and cook for 1 or 2 minutes.
3. Add the mayonnaise and stir well to combine.
4. Split the pasta into 2 plates. Top with the salmon.

9. PALMINI PASTA IN PESTO SAUCE

Serves 4

Nutrition per serving:
665 calories

14 g Protein | 5 g Carbohydrates | 69 g Fat

Total Time: 6 minutes
  Prep: 5 minutes (plus 45 minutes waiting time)
  Cook: 1 minute

INGREDIENTS:

- Palmini, rinsed, 1 can
- Almond milk for soaking, unsweetened, 1 cup
- Basil leaves, 2 cups
- Parmesan cheese, grated, ½ cup
- Pine nuts, ½ cup
- Garlic, 3 cloves
- Salt
- Pepper

PROCEDURE:

1. Soak the palmini in the almond milk for 45 minutes.
2. In a blender, process the basil, Parmesan cheese, pine nuts, and garlic until you get a smooth sauce. Season the sauce with salt and pepper.
3. Cook the palmini over medium heat in a skillet just enough to heat through (about a minute).
4. Top with the pesto sauce.

10. GOLDEN CARBONARA WITH SAGE AND BACON

Serves 2

Nutrition per serving:
397 calories

18 g Protein | 17 g Carbohydrates | 29 g Fat

Total Time: 30 minutes
Prep: 10 minutes
Cook: 20 minutes

INGREDIENTS:

- Butternut squash, diced, 1 cup
- Cauliflower florets, 2 cups
- Bacon, diced, 1 ½ cups
- Zucchini, spiralized, 3 cups
- Turmeric, ½ tsp
- Salt
- Butter, 3 tbsp
- Chicken broth, ¼ cup
- Sage leaves, handful

PROCEDURE:

1. Steam the butternut squash and cauliflower until cooked through.
2. Fry the bacon until crisp and golden in color. Set aside.
3. In the same frying pan, fry the sage leaves in bacon fat. Set the sage leaves aside with the bacon.
4. Cook the zucchini noodles in the same frying pan. Set aside.
5. Put the cooked cauliflower and butternut squash in a food processor. Add the butter, salt, turmeric, and 2 tablespoons of the chicken broth. Blend together until you get a smooth, creamy sauce. Add broth if necessary so you get the consistency you like.
6. Divide the zucchini noodles into 2 plates. Top with the sauce. Sprinkle with bacon bits and sage.

11. SPAGHETTI SQUASH BOLOGNESE

Serves 8

Nutrition per serving:
440 calories

20 g Protein | 12 g Carbohydrates | 34 g Fat

Total Time: 1 hour, 30 minutes
   Prep: 10 minutes
   Cook: 1 hr, 20 minutes

INGREDIENTS:

- Ground beef, 2 lb
- Coconut oil, 1/4 cup (for the beef)
- Onion, diced, 1
- Diced tomato, 1 14.5-oz can
- Fresh basil, chopped, 1 cup
- Garlic, minced, 8 cloves
- Spaghetti squash, 1 whole (about 5 lbs in weight)
- Coconut oil, 2 tbsp (for the spaghetti squash)
- Salt
- Pepper

PROCEDURE:

1. Heat ¼ cup coconut oil. Add the garlic and diced onion and sauté.
2. Add the ground beef and cook until it turns brown.
3. Add the tomatoes and lower the heat. Simmer for an hour, stirring every now and then to make sure that the beef does not stick to the bottom of the pan. Season the meat with salt and pepper. Set aside.
4. Cut the spaghetti squash in half and take the seeds out. Gently rub the insides of the squash with coconut oil with your hands.
5. Cover each portion with paper towel and cook in the microwave oven for 6 or 7 minutes each.
6. Using a fork, scrape the spaghetti squash to form the noodles.
7. Arrange the noodles on a plate. Top with the sauce.

12. CHORIZO PASTA

Serves 2

Nutrition per serving:
339 calories

     13 g Protein | 4 g Carbohydrates | 30 g Fat

Total Time: 30 minutes
 Prep: 10 minutes
 Cook: 20 minutes

INGREDIENTS

Pasta:

- Shirataki noodles, 8 oz

Sauce:

- Coconut oil, 1 tsp
- Chorizo sausage, sliced
- Ground cumin, 1 tsp
- Pureed tomatoes, 1 cup
- Heavy cream, ½ cup

Garnish:

- Basil leaves

PROCEDURE:

1. Heat the oil in a saucepan. Add the chorizo and cook until it turns brown. Season the chorizo with cumin.
2. Add the tomato puree and the heavy cream. Cover the saucepan with the lid and let the sauce simmer for a few minutes.
3. In the meantime, cook the pasta per instructions on the package. Drain on a colander.
4. Add the pasta to the sauce, gently toss, and allow the pasta to absorb the flavors.
5. Transfer to a serving dish. Garnish with basil.

13. PASTA WITH GARLICKY CHICKEN MEATBALLS

Serves 4

Nutrition per serving:
457 calories

32 g Protein | 5 g Carbohydrates | 35 g Fat

Total Time: 35 minutes
   Prep: 10 minutes
   Cook: 25 minutes

INGREDIENTS:

Meatballs:

- Ground chicken, 1 lb
- Garlic, minced, 2 cloves
- Egg, beaten, 1
- Parmesan cheese, grated, ½ cup (Add more if using for garnish)
- Red pepper flakes, crushed, ¼ tsp
- Salt
- Pepper
- Olive oil, 2 tbsp (for cooking the meatballs)

Pasta:

- Zucchini noodles, 1 lb
- Butter, 4 tbsp
- Garlic, minced, 3 cloves
- Juice of half a lemon

PROCEDURE:

1. Combine all the ingredients for the meatballs in a large mixing bowl. Mix gently but thoroughly.
2. Scoop out a tablespoon of the mixture and form into a ball. Do the same with the rest of the mixture.
3. Heat olive oil in a skillet and cook the meatballs. Turn them so they turn a beautiful golden brown on all sides and are cooked through. Set the meatballs aside. Use a paper towel to wipe down your skillet.
4. In the same skillet, melt butter and cook the garlic for a minute or until it releases its fragrance.

5. Toss the zucchini noodles in the garlic butter. Add the lemon juice. Mix to combine gently.
6. Transfer the zucchini noodles on a serving platter. Top with meatballs. Garnish with Parmesan cheese, if desired.

14. ALMOND FLOUR PASTA

Serves 4

Nutrition per serving:
312 calories

17 g Protein | 8 g Carbohydrates | 23 g Fat

Total Time: 40 minutes
   Prep: 35 minutes
   Cook: 5 minutes

INGREDIENTS:

Pasta:

- Almond flour (finely blanched), 2 cups
- Tapioca starch, 2 tbsp
- Egg, 2
- Water, ¼ cup

Sauce:

- Almond milk (unsweetened), ½ cup
- Heavy cream, ½ cup
- Parmesan cheese, grated, ½ cup
- Cheddar cheese (sharp), grated, ¼ cup
- Nutmeg, pinch
- Salt
- Pepper

PROCEDURE:

1. Make the pasta.
   In a large bowl, put all the dry ingredients for the pasta.
   Move the ingredients to the sides to make a well in the middle of the bowl. Put the water and eggs in this well.
   Using a fork, gently combine all the ingredients to form dough.
   Prepare a clean working surface and dust it with tapioca starch.
   Move the dough to this surface. Knead the dough to a smooth consistency. Let it rest for half an hour.
   Roll the dough out into a thin layer.
   Use a sharp knife to slice the dough into pasta strips. Set the strips aside to dry while you prepare the sauce.

2. Make the sauce.

   Pour the heavy cream and almond milk into a saucepan and heat. When the milk/cream starts to simmer, add the cheeses.

   Season the sauce with salt, pepper, and nutmeg. Stir until the cheeses melt. Set aside.
3. Assemble the dish.

   Boil water. Add salt and a little oil. Cook the pasta in the boiling water for about a minute.

   Put the cooked pasta in the saucepan with the sauce. Stir gently so that the sauce coats the pasta.

   Transfer to a serving dish.

15. SHRIMP SCAMPI

Serves 2

Nutrition per serving:
334 calories

48 g Protein | 8 g Carbohydrates | 13 g Fat

Total Time: 30 minutes
Prep: 20 minutes
Cook: 10 minutes

INGREDIENTS:

- Summer squash, 2
- Butter, 2 tbsp
- Chicken broth, ¼ cup
- Lemon juice, 2 tbsp
- Red chili flakes, 1/8 tsp
- Salt
- Pepper
- Shrimp, deveined, 1 lb
- Parsley, chopped, 2 tbsp
- Garlic, minced, 1 clove

PROCEDURE:

1. Use a spiralizer to cut the squash into noodles.
2. Lay the noodles on paper towels and dust with salt. Set aside for 20-30 minutes. The salt will draw out the water from the squash.
3. Gently wring the noodles to remove excess moisture. Set the noodles aside.
4. In a saucepan, melt the butter. Brown the garlic. Add the broth, juice and red chili flakes. Let the mixture come to a light boil then add the shrimp.
5. When the shrimp starts to turn pink, lower the heat. Season the shrimp with salt and pepper.
6. Add the noodles and parsley and gently stir to coat the noodles with the scampi sauce.
7. Serve warm.

16. LEMON CHICKEN PASTA

Serves 3

Nutrition per serving:
325 calories

39 g Protein | 3 g Carbohydrates | 16 g Fat

Total Time: 25 minutes
Prep: 5 minutes
Cook: 20 minutes

INGREDIENTS:

- Shirataki noodles, cooked, 2 7-oz packs
- Chicken breast, diced, 1 lb
- Olive oil, 1 tbsp
- Garlic, minced, 1 clove
- Dried oregano, ½ tsp
- Salt, ½ tsp
- Juice of 1 lemon
- Butter, 2 tbsp
- Xanthan gum, ¼ tsp

Garnish:

- Zest of 1 lemon
- Oregano leaves, chopped, 2 tbsp

PROCEDURE:

1. Heat a large skillet to medium heat. Add the olive oil.
2. Sauté the chicken in the oil and add salt, garlic, and oregano. Cook for 15 or 20 minutes. Transfer the chicken to a plate.
3. De-glaze the skillet by adding the lemon juice.
4. Add the butter. Add the xanthan gum.
5. Put the Shirataki noodles and chicken in the skillet and toss together.
6. Transfer the pasta to a serving dish. Garnish with oregano and lemon zest.

17. EASY AGLIO E OLIO

Serves 2

Nutrition per serving:
315 calories

9 g Protein | 3 g Carbohydrates | 31 g Fat

Total Time: 20 minutes
  Prep: 5 minutes
  Cook: 15 minutes

INGREDIENTS:

- Shirataki noodles, cooked, 10 oz
- Olive oil, ¼ cup
- Garlic, minced, 4 cloves
- Parmesan cheese, grated, ¼ cup

PROCEDURE:

1. Heat olive oil in a skillet.
2. Add the minced garlic and cook until the garlic turns golden in color and releases its fragrance.
3. Add the noodles to the skillet and toss in the garlic oil for about a minute.
4. Transfer to a serving platter and top with the grated Parmesan cheese.

18. TOMATOES AND MUSSELS WITH SHIRATAKI NOODLES

Serves 2

Nutrition per serving:
306 calories

> *26 g Protein | 12 g Carbohydrates | 17 g Fat*

Total Time: 35 minutes
Prep: 5 minutes
Cook: 30 minutes

INGREDIENTS:

- Olive oil, 2 tbsp (divided)
- Garlic, minced, 2 cloves
- Chili powder, 1 tsp
- Tomato, finely chopped, 1
- Mussels (raw), washed and cleaned, about 12 pieces
- Vegetable stock, ¾ cup
- Fresh parsley, 2 tsp
- Shirataki noodles, cooked, 10 oz

PROCEDURE:

1. Make the tomato mixture. Sauté the garlic in a tablespoon of olive oil, add the salt, chili powder, and tomatoes and simmer for 8-10 minutes. Set aside.
2. In another pan, heat the remaining tablespoon of olive oil. Add the mussels and cook with the lid on for 5 minutes.
3. Drain the mussel liquid. Steam the mussels again for another 2 minutes. Drain yet again.
4. Put in the vegetable stock, as well as half of the tomato sauce. Stir to combine.
5. Add the Shirataki noodles and the last half of the tomato sauce. Gently fold to combine and cook for about a minute.
6. Serve warm.

19. CHICKEN LAZONE PASTA

Serves 4

Nutrition per serving:
561 calories

34 g Protein | 5 g Carbohydrates | 44 g Fat

Total Time: 30 minutes
   Prep: 5 minutes
   Cook: 25 minutes

INGREDIENTS:

- Smoked paprika, 2 tsp
- Onion powder, ½ teaspoon
- Garlic powder, ½ teaspoon
- Dried oregano, ½ teaspoon
- Cayenne pepper, ½ teaspoon
- Dried basil, ½ teaspoon
- Salt and pepper to taste
- Chicken tenderloins, 8 pieces (about 1 ¼ lb)
- Olive oil, 1 tbsp
- Butter, 5 tbsp (divided)
- Zucchini noodles, 1 ¼ lb
- Whipping cream, 1 cup
- xanthan gum, ¼ tsp

Garnish (optional):

- Parsley (fresh), chopped

PROCEDURE:

1. In a mixing bowl, combine all the seasonings.
2. Add the chicken tenders and olive oil and gently stir to combine.
3. Get a large skillet. Melt 3 tablespoons of butter using medium-high heat.
4. Add half of the seasoned chicken tenders and cook for about 3 or 4 minutes on each side. Set the cooked chicken tenders aside.
5. Do the same with the remaining chicken tenders. Set the cooked chicken tenders aside.
6. In the same skillet, put the remaining 2 tablespoons of butter. Add the cream. Stir to incorporate the brown bits from the chicken tenders.

47

7. Thicken the sauce by putting in the xanthan gum.
8. Check the seasoning for taste. Add more salt or pepper if desired.
9. Toss the zucchini noodles in the sauce.
10. Transfer the noodles to a serving platter. Top with the chicken tenders.

20. SALMON AND AVOCADO PASTA

Serves 1

Nutrition per serving:
320 calories

29 g Protein | 16 g Carbohydrates | 20 g Fat

Time: 15 minutes
Prep. 5 minutes
Cook: 10 minutes

INGREDIENTS:

- Wild salmon (skinless), 4 oz
- Pesto sauce, 1 tbsp
- Salt, to taste
- Pepper, to taste
- Zucchini noodles, 1 cup
- ¼ of an avocado, sliced,
- Cherry tomatoes, halved, 3

PROCEDURE:

1. Pre-heat your oven to 425°F.
2. Put the salmon on a paper-lined baking sheet. Use salt and pepper to season.
3. Bake for 8 to 10 minutes or until the salmon turns opaque and is cooked through.
4. In the meantime, toss the zucchini noodles in the pesto sauce.
5. Transfer the noodles to a serving platter. Top with the baked salmon. Garnish with tomatoes and avocado slices.

CHAPTER 5

20 KETO PIZZA RECIPES

1. KETO PIZZA CRUST

Note: You can use the procedure outlined below to prepare the crust for other pizza crust recipes that use cheese and flour as their main ingredients.

Some recipes will have fewer ingredients for the crust. This is okay; just follow the general procedure.

If the recipe calls for just cheese and flour, for example, you can just melt the cheese in the microwave and then incorporate the flour after. If the recipe calls for cheese (or different types of cheeses), flour, and other ingredients, melt the cheese(s) and then add in the flour, as well as the other ingredients.

The steps outlined in this recipe will give you a general idea about how to go about forming, shaping, and baking the crust.

Serves 6

Nutrition (for the crust only) per serving:
203 calories

11 g Protein | 4 g Carbohydrates | 17 g Fat

Total Time: 40 minutes
Prep: 10 minutes
Cook: 30 minutes

INGREDIENTS:

Crust:

- Mozzarella cheese, grated, 1 ½ cups
- Cream cheese, 2 tbsp
- Almond flour, ¾ cup
- Egg, 1

- Dried rosemary, ½ tsp dried rosemary
- Salt, ½ tsp
- Garlic powder, ½ tsp
- Ground pepper, 1/4 tsp

Choice of toppings (mushrooms, pepperoni, olives, cherry tomatoes, bell pepper)

PROCEDURE:

1. Pre-heat your oven to 400°F.
2. Put the cheeses in a microwave-safe bowl. Cook in the microwave oven for a minute, using the high setting. Stir the cheeses and return to the microwave oven to cook in 30-second bursts until the cheeses melt fully.
3. Add the flour, egg, dried rosemary, and salt, mix, and knead thoroughly using your hands, the food processor, or the stand mixer.
4. Put the dough in between 2 sheets of parchment paper and roll out the pizza dough to form a round pizza base that is about 8 or 10 inches in diameter. Use your hands or a rolling pin to do this. Remove the top sheet.
5. Use a fork to poke holes on the base.
6. Put the dough (including the parchment paper at its base) on a baking tray and bake for 12 to 15 minutes until the dough turns golden brown.
7. If you want a firm, crisp crust, flip the pizza over and cook for 3 to 5 minutes more.
8. Let the crust stand for a couple of minutes.
9. Add your choice of toppings. Return the pizza to the oven to cook for 5-10 more minutes to heat the pre-cooked toppings and melt the cheese.

2. CHEESE-GARLIC PIZZA

Serves 8

Nutrition per serving:
184 calories

>   *12 g Protein | 4 g Carbohydrates | 14 g Fat*

Total Time: 40 minutes
  Prep: 10 minutes
  Cook: 30 minutes

INGREDIENTS:

Crust:

- Mozzarella cheese, shredded, 1 ½ cups
- Almond flour, 2/3 cup

Toppings:

- Butter, melted, 2 tsp
- Garlic, minced, 2 cloves
- Mozzarella cheese, shredded, 1 ½ cups

Garnish (optional):

- Extra virgin oil for drizzling on top
- Fresh herbs

PROCEDURE:

1. Refer to the recipe for Keto Pizza Crust. Follow Steps 1 to 8 (but use the crust ingredients for Cheese-Garlic Pizza)
2. Drizzle with butter. Add the garlic and mozzarella cheese and put the pizza back in the oven to bake for 10 more minutes.
3. Drizzle with extra virgin olive oil and garnish with fresh herbs, if desired.
4. Serve the pizza hot.

3. BASIL-BELL PEPPER PIZZA

Serves 4

Nutrition per serving:
411 calories

> *22 g Protein | 6 g Carbohydrates | 31 g Fat*

Total Time: 40 minutes
  Prep: 10 minutes
  Cook: 30 minutes

INGREDIENTS:

Crust:

- Mozzarella cheese, 6 oz
- Almond flour, ½ cup
- Parmesan cheese, shredded, 2 tbsp
- Cream cheese, 2 tbsp
- Psyllium husk, 2 tablespoons
- Egg, 1
- Italian seasoning, 1 tsp
- Salt, ½ tsp
- Pepper, ½ tsp

Toppings:

- Marinara sauce (sugar-free), ¼ cup
- Cheddar cheese, grated, 4 ounces
- Tomato, sliced, 1
- Bell pepper, sliced, 1
- Fresh basil, chopped, 2 tbsp

PROCEDURE:

1. Prepare the crust following Steps 1 to 8 as outlined in the recipe for Keto Pizza Crust.
2. Once the crust has cooled a bit, spread the marinara sauce over it. Follow with a sprinkle of cheddar cheese. Top with the slices of tomato, bell pepper, and fresh basil.
3. Bake for another 8-10 minutes.

4. PEPPERONI PIZZA

Serves 2

Nutrition per serving:
611 calories

                    38 g Protein | 20 g Carbohydrates | 42 g Fat

Total Time: 40 minutes
    Prep: 10 minutes
    Cook: 30 minutes

INGREDIENTS:

Crust:

- Cream cheese, 2 tbsp
- Mozzarella cheese, shredded, 1 ½ cups
- Coconut flour, ⅓ cup
- Eggs, 2

Toppings:

- Marinara sauce (sugar-free), ¼ cup
- Mozzarella cheese, shredded, ½ cup
- Pepperoni, 8 slices

PROCEDURE:

1. Prepare the crust following Steps 1 to 8 as outlined in the recipe for Keto Pizza Crust.
2. Spread the marinara sauce evenly over the crust.
3. Sprinkle the mozzarella cheese over the sauce.
4. Put the slices of pepperoni.
5. Bake the pizza for another 10-12 minutes or until the edges and cheese turn golden brown.

5. PIZZA MARGHERITA

Serves 6

Nutrition per serving:
237 calories

$15\,g\,Protein\ |\ 5\,g\,Carbohydrates\ |\ 17\,g\,Fat$

Total Time: 32 minutes
  Prep: 10 minutes
  Cook: 20 minutes
  Resting time: 2 minutes

INGREDIENTS:

- Keto Pizza Crust (refer to Keto Pizza Crust recipe for ingredients and procedure)

Toppings:

- Tomato sauce, 1/3 cup
- Fresh mozzarella, sliced into 4 pieces, 4 oz
- Fresh basil, 4 leaves

Garnish (optional):

- Parmesan cheese, grated
- Dried oregano or other Italian herbs of choice

PROCEDURE:

1. Prepare the crust according to instructions outlined in the recipe for Keto Pizza Crust.
2. Cover the pizza crust with the tomato sauce. Add the mozzarella cheese.
3. Bake for 8 minutes or until the cheese melts.
4. Top with the basil leaves.
5. Garnish with parmesan cheese and seasoning of choice, if desired.

6. PIZZA WITH EGG-CHEESE CRUST

Nutrition per serving:
1043 calories

53 g Protein | 6 g Carbohydrates | 90 g Fat

Total Time: 30 minutes
  Prep: 5 minutes
  Cook: 25 minutes

INGREDIENTS:

Crust:

- Eggs, 4
- Cheese (provolone or mozzarella), shredded, 6 oz

Topping:

- Tomato sauce (unsweetened), 3 tbsp
- Dried oregano, 1 tsp
- Cheese (Cheddar), grated, 5 oz.
- Pepperoni, 1½ oz
- Olives (optional)

For serving:

- Leafy greens, 2 oz
- Olive oil, 4 tbsp
- Salt, to taste
- Black pepper, to taste

PROCEDURE:

1. Pre-heat your oven to 400°F. Line a baking sheet with parchment paper.
2. Place the eggs and the cheese in a bowl and stir to combine thoroughly.
3. Transfer the batter to the baking sheet. Use a spatula to form a large rectangular pizza crust.
4. Bake the crust for about 15 minutes or until it turns a pale golden brown.
5. Take the crust out of the oven and let it cool for a couple of minutes. Switch the oven up to 450°F.

6. Top the crust with tomato sauce, oregano, olives, pepperoni, and cheese.
7. Bake the crust again until the cheese turns bubbly (about 5 or 10 minutes).
8. Serve the pizza with the salad.

7. CAULIFLOWER-SPINACH PIZZA

Serves 2

Nutrition per serving:
298 calories

23 g Protein | 9 g Carbohydrates | 18 g Fat

Total Time: 50 minutes
  Prep: 20 minutes
  Cook: 30 minutes

INGREDIENTS:

Crust:

- Cauliflower, finely chopped, 1
- Egg, 1
- Mozzarella cheese (grated), 100 g
- Salt, ½ tsp
- Pepper, ¼ tsp
- Dried oregano, ½ tsp

Toppings:

- Mozzarella cheese, shredded, ¾ cup
- Pecorino Romano cheese, grated, ¼ cup
- Cooked spinach, ½ cup
- Sun-dried tomatoes, chopped, a handful

PROCEDURE:

1. Steam the cauliflower until they are soft.
2. Put the cooked cauliflower on a clean tea towel and gently press to remove all liquid. Getting rid of the liquid ensures that you will have a crisp pizza base.
3. Put the cauliflower in a large bowl. Add the rest of the ingredients and mix thoroughly to form a ball.
4. Put your cauliflower "dough" on a paper-lined baking sheet and press to form a round pizza crust.
5. Spray some olive oil on top. Bake at 350°F for 15-20 minutes or until the crust turns golden. Let the crust cool.

6. Sprinkle mozzarella cheese over the crust. Spread the spinach and tomatoes over the mozzarella cheese. Top with Pecorino Romano. Sprinkle a pinch of salt over the pizza.
7. Return the pizza to the oven and bake for another 5 minutes to allow the cheeses to melt.

8. THIN CRUST PITA BREAD PIZZA

Serves 1

Nutrition per serving:
254 calories

19 g Protein | 8 g Carbohydrates | 16 g Fat

Total Time: 30
  Prep: 10 minutes
  Cook: 20 minutes

INGREDIENTS:

- Pita bread (sugar-free), 1 piece
- Tomato sauce (sugar-free), 2 tbsp
- Garlic powder, 1/8 tsp
- Black pepper, freshly ground, 1/8 tsp
- Chili flakes, 1/8 tsp
- Mozzarella cheese, shredded, 2 oz

Other toppings (optional):

- Avocado slices
- Prosciutto
- Olives
- Pepperoni
- Sriracha

PROCEDURE:

1. Preheat your oven to 450°F.
2. Lightly brush a baking sheet with cooking oil. Put the pita on the baking sheet and toast for a couple of minutes.
3. Take the pita out of the oven. Put the toppings and cheese on it.
4. Return the pita to the oven and toast until the cheese melts.

9. DEEP DISH PIZZA

Serves 8

Nutrition per serving (for the crust):
88 calories

3 g Protein | 4 g Carbohydrates | 6 g Fat

Total Time: 15 minutes
   Prep: 10 minutes
   Cook: 5 minutes

INGREDIENTS:

- Almond flour, 1 cup
- Coconut flour, 3 tbsp
- Xanthan gum, 2 tsp
- Baking powder, 1 tsp
- Active dry yeast, 2 tsp (optional)
- Garlic powder, ¼ tsp (optional)
- Dried basil, ½ tsp
- Salt, ¼ tsp
- Apple cider vinegar, 2 tsp
- Egg, lightly beaten, 1
- Water (as needed), about 3 to 7 tsp

Suggestions for filling:

- Marinara sauce (sugar-free), 1-2 cups
- Mozzarella cheese, shredded, 1-2 cups
- Zucchini, spiralized, 1 cup
- Onions, caramelized
- Salami or pepperoni

PROCEDURE:

1. Put all the dry ingredients for the dough in the food processor. Pulse to combine.
2. Without turning off the food processor, add the apple cider vinegar. Mix thoroughly.
3. Add the egg.
4. Add water gradually until the mixture forms a ball. The dough should be sticky but firm.

5. Use cling film to wrap the dough. Knead the dough through the film for 1-2 minutes until it becomes smooth. (If the dough cracks, put it back in the food processor. Add a teaspoon of water or more as needed until you get the right consistency and knead as before).
6. Let the dough rest at room temperature for about 10 minutes while you pre-heat your oven to 350°F.
7. Put the dough in between 2 sheets of parchment paper and roll it out using a rolling pin.
8. Put parchment paper at the bottom of a metal pie pan (8-inch) and transfer the dough to the pan.
9. Tuck in the edges of the dough to get a thick edge.
10. Bake the dough for 10-12 minutes until it sets fully and starts to turn a light golden color.
11. Take the crust out of the oven. Put on the toppings of your choice one layer at a time.
12. Return the pie to the oven. Bake for 25 minutes or so. If the edges of the pie turn prematurely brown, loosely cover the dish with aluminum foil.
13. Garnish the pie with fresh basil, if desired.

10. CARAMELIZED ONIONS PIZZA

Serves 8

Nutrition per serving:
322 calories

> *9 g Protein | 12 g Carbohydrates | 30 g Fat*

Total Time: 1 hour and 20 minutes
Prep: 30 minutes
Cook: 50 minutes

INGREDIENTS:

For the caramelized onions:

- Onion (white), sliced thinly, 1 cup
- Olive oil, 2 tbsp
- Salt, ¼ tsp

For the sauce:

- Mayonnaise, ¼ cup
- Cashew milk (unsweetened) 2 tbsp
- Nutritional yeast (optional), 1 tbsp

For the crust:

- Almond flour, 2 cups
- Coconut flour, ½ cup
- Baking powder, 1 tbsp
- Salt, ½ tsp
- Italian seasoning, ½ tsp
- Whites of 4 eggs
- Avocado oil, ¼ cup
- Cashew milk (unsweetened), ¼ cup

Garnish (optional):

- Fresh basil
- Ground pepper

PROCEDURE:

1. Prepare the caramelized onions.

   Cook the onions in olive oil. Sprinkle with salt. Cook for about 15-20 minutes or until soft and gold in color. Set aside.

2. Prepare the sauce.

   Whisk all the sauce ingredients until you get a smooth consistency. Set aside.

3. Prepare the crust.

   Whisk all the dry ingredients for the crust in a large bowl. Add the wet ingredients and stir until a sticky ball of dough forms.

   Divide the dough into 2.

   Brush a big piece of parchment paper with oil. Turn the 1st piece of dough into the parchment paper and form into a disk.

   Cover the dough with parchment paper and use a rolling pin to roll it out into a 10-inch circle. Do the same with the other piece of dough. Discard the top parchment paper.

   Set the dough (and the bottom parchment paper) on a baking sheet. Bake for 20-25 minutes or until the crust is firm and the edges are golden brown.

4. Put the pizza sauce on the pizza. Top with the caramelized onions. Bake for 5 to 8 minutes.

5. Garnish with chopped fresh basil and freshly-ground pepper, if desired.

11. PORTOBELLO PIZZA

Serves 4

Nutrition per serving:
339 calories

> *10 g Protein | 4 g Carbohydrates | 32 g Fat*

Total Time: 30 minutes
  Prep: 10 minutes
  Cook: 20 minutes

INGREDIENTS:

- Portobello mushrooms, 4
- Olive oil, 6 tbsp
- Salt
- Pepper
- Tomato, sliced very thinly to make 12 to 16 wedges, 1
- Fresh basil, chopped, ¼ cup
- Mozzarella cheese, cubed, 4 oz
- Pepperoni, 20 slices

PROCEDURE:

1. Pre-heat your oven to "broil."
2. Remove the meat from the Portobello mushrooms so only the shells remain.
3. Divide the 3 tablespoons of olive oil among the mushrooms and gently rub in. Sprinkle salt and pepper over the mushrooms.
4. Put the mushrooms in the oven and broil for 4 minutes. Flip over and broil the other side.
5. Put the tomato slices on top of the mushrooms. Sprinkle basil on top.
6. Add the pepperoni and mozzarella.
7. Put the mushrooms back into the oven and broil for 3-4 minutes or until the cheese melts.

12. QUICK FRIED-CRUST PIZZA

Serves 1

Nutrition per serving:
459 calories

> *27 g Protein | 3 g Carbohydrates | 35 g Fat*

Total Time: 10
  Prep: 5 minutes
  Cook: 5 minutes

INGREDIENTS:

Crust:

- Eggs, 2
- Parmesan cheese, grated, 2 tbsp
- Psyllium husk powder, 1 tbsp
- Italian seasoning, ½ tsp
- Salt
- Bacon fat (for frying), 2 tsp

Toppings:

- Tomato sauce (sugar-free), 3 tbsp
- Mozzarella cheese, shredded, 1 ½ oz
- Fresh basil, chopped, 1 tbsp

PROCEDURE:

1. Use a blender to combine all the ingredients for the crust.
2. Heat the bacon fat in a pan. Put the crust mixture in, spreading it out to form a circle, and fry.
3. When the edges start to turn brown, flip the crust over and cook the other side for 40-60 seconds.
4. Spread the tomato sauce over the crust. Add the cheese. Broil for 2 minutes or until the cheese melts.
5. Garnish with fresh basil.

13. MEAT LOVERS PIZZA

Serves 1

Nutrition per serving:
337 calories

36 g Protein | 3 g Carbohydrates | 22 g Fat

Total Time: 40 minutes
Prep: 15 minutes
Cook: 25 minutes

INGREDIENTS:

Crust:

- Bacon, 5 slices

Toppings:

- Red onion, sliced, 1/8 tsp
- Pizza sauce (sugar-free), 2 tbsp
- Mozzarella cheese, grated, 2 tbsp
- Tomatoes (Roma), sliced, seeds removed, ½ oz
- Parmesan cheese, grated, 1 tbsp
- Italian chicken sausage (hot), 1 oz
- Red pepper flakes, 1 tsp

PROCEDURE:

1. Pre-heat your oven to 400°F.
2. Form the pizza "crust" by weaving together the bacon slices.
3. Bake the bacon crust for 10 to 15 minutes or until you get the level of crispness you want.
4. Remove the bacon crust from the oven and drain on paper towels to remove the excess bacon grease.
5. Put the toppings on top of the crust.
6. Return the pizza to the oven and bake for another 10-12 minutes.
7. Top with red pepper flakes before serving.

14. WHITE PIZZA

Serves 2

Nutrition per serving:
1094 calories

36 g Protein | 11 g Carbohydrates | 100 g Fat

Total Time: 30 minutes
Prep: 10 minutes
Cook: 20 minutes

INGREDIENTS:

Crust:

- Eggs, 2½ cup
- Crème fraîche, ½ cup
- Almond flour, ¾ cup
- Psyllium husk powder, 1 tbsp
- Baking powder, 1 tsp
- Salt, ½ tsp

Topping:

- Crème fraîche, ½ cup
- Mozzarella cheese, shredded, 3 oz
- Parmesan cheese, grated, 2 oz
- Dried rosemary, 1 tsp
- Black pepper, 1/8 tsp

PROCEDURE:

1. Pre-heat your oven to 350°F. Prepare a parchment-paper lined baking sheet.
2. Whisk the eggs and the crème fraîche together. Add the other ingredients for the crust and stir until well-combined. Set aside to rest for 5 minutes.
3. Transfer the batter to the baking sheet. Use a spatula or a rolling pin to spread the batter to form a pizza crust that is no more than half an inch thick.
4. Bake the crust for 10-12 minutes or until light golden in color.
5. Let the crust cool a bit.
6. When the crust is cool enough, flip it upside down.
7. Top the crust with crème fraîche. Add the cheese, as well as the pepper and rosemary.

8. Put the pizza back in the oven and bake for 5-10 minutes longer.
9. Sprinkle with grated parmesan cheese and serve.

15. CHICKEN BBQ PIZZA

Serves 4

Nutrition per serving:
357 calories

24 g Protein | 3 g Carbohydrates | 25 g Fat

Total Time: 20 minutes
Prep: 5 minutes
Cook: 15 minutes

INGREDIENTS:

Crust:

- Eggs, 6
- Parmesan cheese, 6 tbsp
- Psyllium husk powder, 3 tbsp
- Italian seasoning, ½ tsp
- Salt
- Pepper

Toppings:

- Cheddar cheese, 4 oz
- Rotisserie chicken, shredded, 6 oz
- Mayonnaise, 1 tbsp
- BBQ sauce (store-bought, sugar-free), 4 tbsp
- Tomato sauce (sugar-free), 4 tbsp

PROCEDURE:

1. Pre-heat your oven to 425°F.
2. Use a blender to thoroughly mix all the ingredients for the crust.
3. Spread dough out in the form of a circle on a baking sheet lined with parchment paper or on a silicon baking mat.
4. Bake the crust in the oven for 10 minutes.
5. Flip the crust over.
6. Put the toppings and return to the oven to broil for another 3 or 5 minutes.

16. MEATZA PIZZA

Serves 4

Nutrition per serving:
456 calories

41 g Protein | 4 g Carbohydrates | 28 g Fat

Total Time: 40 minutes
  Prep: 15 minutes
  Cook: 25 minutes

INGREDIENTS:

Crust:

- Ground beef, 1 lb
- Dried basil, 1 tsp
- Dried oregano, 1 tsp
- Salt, ½ tsp
- Ground pepper, to taste

Toppings:

- Wild mushrooms, sliced, 2 cups
- Butter, 2 tbsp
- Garlic, crushed, 2 cloves
- Spinach, fresh, 7 oz-package
- Pesto sauce, 2 tbsp
- Mozzarella cheese, shredded, ¾ cup

PROCEDURE:

1. Pre-heat your oven to 400°F.
2. In a mixing bowl, combine all the ingredients for the pizza "crust."
3. Use your hands to form the ground beef mixture into a crust that is about ½" thick.
4. Put the crust on a parchment paper-lined baking tray.
5. Bake in the oven for 10-15 minutes.
6. In the meantime, get the toppings ready.
7. Let the butter melt on a large skillet. Add the garlic and sauté for a minute.
8. Add the sliced mushrooms and cook for 5-7 minutes, stirring every now and then.

9. Add the spinach and cook for another minute.
10. Season the toppings with salt and pepper.
11. Set aside.
12. Take the cooked meat crust out of the oven. Top with the pesto sauce, half of the cheese, and the mushroom-spinach toppings. Sprinkle the remaining mozzarella cheese on top.
13. Cook the pizza for another 5 minutes or until the cheese melts.

17. SHEET PAN PIZZA

Serves 8

Nutrition per serving:
359 calories

> *29 g Protein | 13 g Carbohydrates | 16 g Fat*

Total Time: 1 hr, 25 minutes
  Prep: 5 minutes
  Cook: 50 minutes
  Chilling time: 30 minutes

INGREDIENTS:

Crust:

- Italian sausage, sweet type, casings removed, ½ lb
- Cream cheese, 2 tbsp
- Almond flour, 1 cup
- Coconut flour, ¼ cup
- Mozzarella cheese, grated, 1 ½ cups
- Parmesan cheese, grated, ¼ cup freshly
- Eggs, 2

Sautéed Vegetable Topping:

- Olive oil, 1 tbsp
- Onion, sliced, 1
- Bell pepper, sliced, 1
- Baby spinach, 8 oz
- Garlic, crushed, 2 tbsp

- Pizza sauce (sugar-free), ½ cup
- Cheddar cheese, grated, ½ cup
- Mozzarella cheese, shredded, 2 cups

PROCEDURE:

1. Pre-heat your oven to 375°F. Lightly oil a 13x9" sheet pan.
2. Combine all the ingredients for the crust.
3. Press the sausage pizza crust evenly into the pan. Refrigerate for 30 minutes so the mixture firms up nicely before baking.

4. Bake the pizza for 12-15 minutes, turning the pan after the first 6-8 minutes.
5. While the crust is in the oven, cook the onions and bell peppers in olive oil for 10 minutes. Put in the spinach and cook until wilted (about a minute). Add the garlic. Set aside.
6. When the sausage crust is cooked, spread the pizza sauce over it. Add the sautéed vegetables. Top with the cheeses.
7. Return to the oven and cook for an additional 25 minutes or until the cheeses melt.

18. CHICKEN-CRUST PIZZA

Serves 8

Nutrition per serving:
172 calories

14 g Protein | 1 g Carbohydrates | 13 g Fat

Total Time: 50
Prep: 5 minutes
Cook: 45 minutes

INGREDIENTS:

Crust:

- Ground chicken, 1 lb
- Mozzarella cheese, shredded, 1 cup
- Egg, 1
- Dried oregano, 1 tsp
- Salt, ¼ tsp
- Black pepper, ¼ tsp

Toppings:

- Butter, 2 tbsp
- Celery, diced finely, 1 stalk
- Sour cream, 1 tbsp
- Hot sauce or cayenne pepper sauce, 3 tbsp
- Blue cheese, crumbled, 1 oz
- Green onion, chopped, 1 stalk

PROCEDURE:

1. Pre-heat your oven to 400°F.
2. In a large mixing bowl, combine ground chicken, half of the mozzarella cheese, egg, and seasonings thoroughly to form the pizza base.
3. Put the ground chicken mixture on a parchment paper-lined baking sheet or pizza pan. Spread the mixture out with the back of a large spoon to form a circle that is about ¼" thick.
4. Bake the base for 25 to 30 minutes or until the crust cooks through and turns golden brown in color.
5. In the meantime, put the butter on a skillet to melt. Add the celery and cook for about 1-2 minutes. Set aside.

6. Mix 2 tablespoons of the hot sauce or cayenne pepper sauce and sour cream in a small bowl.
7. Once the pizza crust is baked, spread the hot sauce/sour cream mixture over its base. Add the onion, crumbled blue cheeses, and the remaining mozzarella.
8. Return to the oven to cook for 10-12 more minutes or until the cheese melts.
9. Drizzle with the remaining tablespoon of hot sauce. Garnish with green onion.

19. CHAFFLE PIZZA

Serves 2

Nutrition per serving:
241 calories

17 g Protein | 4 g Carbohydrates | 18 g Fat

Total Time: 20 minutes
Prep: 5 minutes
Cook: 15 minutes

INGREDIENTS:

Batter:

- Coconut flour, 1 tsp
- Egg white, 1
- Mozzarella cheese, shredded, ½ cup
- Cream cheese, softened, 1 tsp
- Baking powder, ¼ tsp
- Italian seasoning, 1/8 tsp
- Garlic powder, 1/8 tsp
- Salt

Toppings:

- Marinara sauce (sugar-free), 3 tsp
- Pepperoni, 6 slices - cut in half to make 12 pieces
- Parmesan cheese, grated, 1 tbsp
- Mozzarella cheese, shredded, ½ cup
- Basil seasoning, ¼ tsp

PROCEDURE:

1. Pre-heat your oven to 400°F. Plug in your waffle maker and pre-heat.
2. Combine all the ingredients thoroughly to make the batter.
3. Cook half of the batter in the waffle maker for 3 minutes or until the chaffle is done.
4. Gently take the cooked chaffle out of the waffle maker. Cook the second half of the batter.
5. Top both chaffles with the marinara sauce, pepperoni slices, and cheeses.

6. Bake in the oven for 5 minutes or until the cheese bubbles and melts.
7. Top with basil seasoning.

20. TORTILLA PIZZA

Serves 4

Nutrition per serving:
411 calories

> *22 g Protein | 7 g Carbohydrates | 34 g Fat*

Total Time: 20 minutes
  Prep: 5 minutes
  Cook: 15 minutes

INGREDIENTS:

Tortillas:

- Eggs, 2
- Egg whites, 2
- Cream cheese, 6 oz
- Salt, ¼ tsp
- Psyllium husk powder, 1 tsp
- Coconut flour, 1 tbsp

Toppings:

- Tomato sauce (sugar-free), ½ cup
- Cheese, grated, 8 oz
- Dried oregano or dried basil, 2 tsp
- Salt, to taste
- Black pepper, to taste

PROCEDURE:

1. Pre-heat your oven to 400°F. Line 2 baking sheets with parchment paper. Set aside.
2. Make the tortillas.
3. In a small bowl, combine the psyllium husk, salt, and coconut flour. Set aside.
4. With a hand mixer, whisk together egg whites and eggs until the mixture turns fluffy.
5. Add the cream cheese. Continue whisking until you get a smooth batter.
6. Add the flour mixture to the batter gradually, a tablespoon at a time, while whisking.

7. Let the batter rest for a few minutes until it becomes thicker.
8. Transfer the batter to the baking sheets. Use a spatula to form 2 thin rectangles (about ¼" thick or thinner) per baking sheet.
9. Bake the tortillas for about 5 to 7 minutes or until the edges turn light brown.
10. Let the tortillas cool a little.
11. Turn the oven's temperature up to 450°F.
12. Put between 1 and 2 tablespoons of the tomato paste on each tortilla. Spread evenly.
13. Add a sprinkling of salt, pepper, and herbs. Top with the cheese.
14. Bake the pizza for 3-5 minutes or until the cheese melts.

CHAPTER 6

10 KETO ITALIAN DESSERT RECIPES

1. SEMIFREDDO

Serves 10

Nutrition per serving:
194 calories

5 g Protein | 10 g Carbohydrates | 17 g Fat

Total Time: 6 hours, 30 minutes
Prep: 10 minutes
Cook: 20 minutes
Freezing time: 6 hours

INGREDIENTS:

- Eggs, 3
- Yolk of 1 egg
- Almond flour, ¾ cup
- Sweetener (sugar-free), ¾ cup
- Brandy, 2 tbsp (optional)
- Heavy cream, 1 cup
- Vanilla extract, 1 tsp
- Chocolate chips (dark, sugar-free), ½ cup

Garnish (optional):

- Almonds, sliced and toasted

PROCEDURE:

1. Whisk the whole eggs, egg yolk, and sweetener together in a bowl.
2. Put the bowl over a pan of boiling water. Cook just long enough to dissolve the sweetener and to lightly heat the mixture.

3. Off the heat, put in the almond flour, as well as the brandy (optional). Let the mixture cool.
4. In the meantime, use a stand mixer to whisk the heavy cream with the vanilla extract to form soft peaks.
5. Fold in the egg mixture. Fold in the chocolate chips.
6. Pour the semifreddo into a loaf pan lined with plastic wrap.
7. Freeze for 6 hours or overnight, if possible.
8. Take the loaf pan out of the freezer 5 minutes before you serve the semifreddo.
9. Lift the plastic wrap off the pan and flip the semifreddo over to a serving plate.
10. Garnish with almonds, if desired.

2. CANNOLI MOUSSE

Serves 6

Nutrition per serving:
209 calories

5 g Protein | 2 g Carbohydrates | 20 g Fat

Total Time: 1 hr, 5 minutes
    Prep: 5 minutes
    Chilling time: 1 hour

INGREDIENTS:

- Whipping cream (heavy), 1 cup
- Ricotta cheese, 1 cup
- Sweetener (sugar-free), ¼ cup
- Cinnamon, 1 tsp
- Chocolate chips (sugar-free), ½ cup (optional)

PROCEDURE:

1. Whisk the cream. Put aside.
2. Put the cinnamon and sweetener in a blender or food processor and grind until you get the consistency of confectioners' sugar.
3. Put in the ricotta and blend until you get a smooth mixture.
4. Use a spatula to gently fold the whipped cream into the ricotta cheese mixture.
5. Transfer the mousse to individual serving glasses.
6. Chill for an hour.
7. Garnish with chocolate chips before serving, if desired.

3. ALMOND-RICOTTA CAKE

Serves 12

Nutrition per serving:
274 calories

> *9 g Protein | 6 g Carbohydrates | 24 g Fat*

Total Time: 1 hour, 20 minutes
  Prep: 35 minutes
  Cook: 45 minutes

INGREDIENTS:

- Vanilla, ½ tsp
- Butter, softened, ½ cup
- Ricotta cheese, 1 cup
- Eggs, separated, 4
- Sweetener (sugar-free), ¾ cup
- Salt, ¼ tsp
- Almond flour (blanched), 2 ½ cups
- Lemon zest, 1 tsp
- Almond extract, 1 tsp
- Cream of tartar, ½ tsp
- Almond slivers, 1/3 cp

Garnish (optional):

- Confectioners' sugar (sugar free) for dusting

PROCEDURE:

1. Pre-heat your oven to 325°F.
2. Prepare a round 9-inch spring form pan. Grease the sides and bottom.
3. Using a stand mixer, blend together butter, egg yolks, cheese, sweetener, salt, vanilla, and almond extract.
4. Put in the almond flour, as well as the zest, and continue to blend at low speed. Set the mixture aside.
5. In a dry, clean mixing bowl, whip the egg whites and cream of tartar until you get stiff peaks.
6. Combine the egg whites and the almond mixture by gently folding half of the former into the almond mixture. Add the remaining egg whites and continue to fold.

7. Transfer the batter to the spring form pan. Top with almond slivers.
8. Bake for between 40 and 45 minutes or until the edges of the cake turn golden in color. Prick the center of the cake with a toothpick. If no batter sticks to the toothpick, the cake is done.
9. Set the cake aside for 20 minutes to cool.
10. Using a butter knife, gently loosen the edges of the cake. Take the sides of the pan off.
11. Let the cake cool completely. Dust with powdered sugar, if desired.

4. HAZELNUT CREAMS

Serves 2

Nutrition per serving:
539 calories

7 g Protein | 6 g Carbohydrates | 55 g Fat

Total Time: 1 hr, 45 minutes
   Prep: 5 minutes
   Cook: 40 minutes
   Chilling time: 1 hour

INGREDIENTS:

- Egg, 1
- Heavy cream, 1 cup
- Vanilla extract, ½ tsp
- Sweetener (sugar-free), 2 tbsp
- Hazelnut meal, 2 tbsp

Garnish (optional):

- Chocolate (dark, sugar-free), grated

PROCEDURE:

1. Use a stand mixer to whisk the egg to a smooth consistency.
2. Add the heavy cream, vanilla, and sweetener and continue whisking.
3. Stir in the hazelnut meal.
4. Divide the cream mixture into 2 ramekins.
5. Put the ramekins in a pan with deep sides. Fill the pan with boiling water halfway up the ramekins.
6. Put tin foil over the pan to cover it and simmer for about 35 minutes or until the cream sets.
7. Take the ramekins out of the pan and leave at room temperature to cool.
8. Refrigerate for about an hour before serving.
9. Garnish with grated dark chocolate, if desired.

5. CREAMY BERRY MOUSSE

Serves 4

Nutrition per serving:
255 calories

> *2 g Protein | 4 g Carbohydrates | 26 g Fat*

Total Time: 4 hrs, 10 minutes
  Prep: 10 minutes
  Chilling time: 4 hours

INGREDIENTS:

- Whipping cream (heavy), 1 cup
- Pecans, chopped, 1 oz
- Choice of fresh berries (strawberries, blueberries, or raspberries), 1½ oz
- Zest of ¼ lemon
- Vanilla extract, 1/8 tsp

PROCEDURE:

1. Using a hand mixer, whip the cream until it forms soft peaks. Add the vanilla and zest and continue whipping
2. Fold the nuts and berries into the cream.
3. Cover the bowl with plastic wrap and refrigerate for 4 hours or until the mousse firms up.

6. CUTE CANNOLI CUPCAKES

Serves 12

Nutrition per serving:
289 calories

> *9 g Protein | 7 g Carbohydrates | 25 g Fat*

Total Time: 35 minutes
  Prep: 15 minutes
  Chilling time: 20 hours

INGREDIENTS:

Cupcakes:

- Almond flour, 2 cups
- Whey protein powder (unflavored), ¼ cup
- Baking powder, 1/4 cup
- Salt, ¼ tsp
- Butter, softened, 6 tbsp
- Sweetener, equivalent to sugar, granulated, ½ cup
- Eggs, 2
- Vanilla extract, ½ tsp
- Heavy cream, ¼ cup
- Water, ¼ cup

Frosting:

- Ricotta cheese, ¾ cup
- Cream cheese, softened, 4 oz
- Sweetener (liquid or powdered), equivalent to sugar, granulated, 1/3 cup
- Vanilla extract, ¼ tsp
- Heavy cream, 2-4 tbsp

Garnish:

- Chocolate chips (sugar-free), ¼ cup
- Sweetener (sugar-free, powder form), 1 tbsp

PROCEDURE:

1. Pre-heat your oven to 325°F.
2. Line a mini cupcake pan (24-cavity) with silicon liners or cupcake paper liners.

3. Put the flour, whey protein, salt, and baking powder in a bowl. Whisk the ingredients together to mix. Set aside.

4. Using a stand mixer, beat the butter. Gradually add the sweetener. Add the eggs and vanilla extract. Continue beating vigorously until the batter takes on a pale yellow color.

5. Add the flour mixture, followed by the cream and water, whisking to incorporate all the ingredients.

6. Put the batter in the cupcake pan.

7. Bake for 18-20 minutes or until the cupcakes are firm and the tops are a golden color.

8. Let the cupcakes cool to room temperature.

9. Prepare the frosting.

   Use a food processor or blender to blend the ricotta cheese to a smooth consistency. Set aside.

   In a clean, dry stand mixer, whisk the cream cheese with the sweetener until well-incorporated. Add the ricotta cheese and the vanilla extract and continue to whisk.

   Add the heavy cream a tablespoon at a time until the mixture reaches a frosting consistency.

10. Frost the cupcakes.

11. Garnish with chocolate chips and a dusting of the powdered sweetener.

7. PIGNOLI COOKIES

Serves 20

Nutrition per serving:
83 calories

3 g Protein | 2 g Carbohydrates | 7 g Fat

Total Time: 22 minutes
  Prep: 10 minutes
  Cook: 12 minutes

INGREDIENTS:

- Egg, 1
- Erythritol sweetener (granulated), 1 cup (and more if using for garnish)
- Almond extract, 1 tsp
- Salt, pinch
- Almond flour (blanched, superfine), 2 cups
- Pignoli (pine) nuts, 1/3 cup

PROCEDURE:

1. Pre-heat your oven to 325°F. Line a baking sheet with parchment paper.
2. Beat the egg, sweetener, almond extract, and salt together in a mixer.
3. Add the flour. Continue beating until everything is well-incorporated and forms a stiff dough. If the dough turns out too dry, add half or a tablespoon of water to the mixture.
4. Spread out the pignoli nuts on a tray.
5. Get a piece of dough, form it into a 1"-ball and press it against the nuts. Put the cookie (the side with the nuts facing up) on the baking sheet.
6. Do the same with the rest of the dough. The dough should yield about 20 cookies.
7. Using the back of a spoon, flatten each cookie by lightly pressing down on it. This step will also press the nuts down to keep them in place.
8. Bake the pignoli cookies for 12 minutes or just until the tops of

the cookies turn golden brown. Do not over bake if you don't want to end up with dry cookies.

9. Let the cookies cool on a rack.
10. Finish with a dusting of powdered erythritol (optional).

8. STRAWBERRY PANNA COTTA

Serves 4

Nutrition per serving:
330 calories

4 g Protein | 19 g Carbohydrates | 32 g Fat

Total Time: 3 hrs, 15 minutes
  Prep: 10 minutes
  Cook: 5 minutes
  Chilling time: 3 hours

INGREDIENTS:

- Strawberries, chopped, 1 cup
- Whipping cream (heavy), 1 ½ cups
- Sweetener (sugar-free, powder form), 1/3 cup
- Gelatin, 1 ¾ tsp
- Vanilla extract, ½ tsp

PROCEDURE:

1. Use a blender to puree the strawberries.
2. Using a medium saucepan, gently heat the cream. Add the gelatin a little at a time, whisking constantly to incorporate and dissolve the gelatin.
3. Off the heat, whisk in the sweetener and vanilla extract. Fold in the strawberries.
4. Transfer the mixture to 4 dessert cups or ramekins. Put the panna cotta in the refrigerator to set completely (about 2-3 hours).

9. ZABAGLIONE

Serves 2

Nutrition per serving:
69 calories

2 g Protein | 2 g Carbohydrates | 4 g Fat

Total Time: 10 minutes
Prep: 2 minutes
Cook: 8 minutes

INGREDIENTS:

- Yolk of 2 eggs
- Sweetener (sugar-free), 2 tbsp
- Marsala wine, 1 tbsp

Garnish (optional):

- Cocoa powder

PROCEDURE:

1. Beat the egg yolks. Add the wine and sweetener and continue whisking.
2. Transfer the mixture to a saucepan. Over low heat, continue whisking until foam forms.
3. Keep on whisking to thicken the foam.
4. Spoon the frothy custard into small dessert glasses.
5. Garnish with a dusting of cocoa powder, if using.

10. TIRAMISU DESSERT JARS

Serves 6

Nutrition per serving:
460 calories

> *8 g Protein | 6 g Carbohydrates | 45 g Fat*

Total Time: 1 hr, 25 minutes
  Prep: 10 minutes
  Cook: 20 minutes
  Chilling time: 1 hour

INGREDIENTS:

Sponge Base:

- Almond flour, ½ cup
- Coconut flour, 3 tbsp
- Erythritol sweetener (powdered), 2-3 tbsp
- Baking soda, ¼ tsp
- Cream of tartar, 1/3 tsp

- Protein whey powder, 1 ¼ tbsp
- Eggs, 3
- Butter (melted), 2 tbsp
- Almond milk, 3 tbsp

Coffee-Rum Mixture:

- Coffee, (filtered, freshly brewed), ¾ cup

- Rum (dark), ¼ cup
- Erythritol (powdered), 3 tbsp

Mascarpone Cream:

- Mascarpone, ¾ cup

- Heavy cream, ¾ cup

Topping:

- Chocolate (dark), grated, 2 squares

Garnish:

- Cacao powder, 1/3 tsp

PROCEDURE:

1. Make the base.

    Pre-heat your oven to 375°F. Line a 9 x 6" baking tray with parchment paper.

    Separate the eggs.

    In a mixing bowl, cream the egg yolks. Add the sweetener and continue creaming until the mixture turns a light and pale yellow.

    In another bowl, use an electric mixer to whisk the egg whites to soft peaks consistency.

    Fold the whites carefully into the yolks, seeing to it that the whites do not deflate. Set aside.

    Make the flour mixture by putting and mixing all the dry ingredients in a bowl.

    Fold the flour mixture, butter, and almond milk into the egg mixture.

    Transfer the batter to the baking tray. Use a spatula to make the top smooth and even.

    Bake the cake in the oven until it turns a golden color (about 18 to 20 minutes). Check for doneness by lightly pricking the center of the cake with a toothpick. If the toothpick comes out with no batter sticking to it, the cake is ready.

    Let the cake cool.

    Slice into about 40 small squares.

2. Make the coffee-rum mixture.

    Mix the coffee, rum and sweetener in a small bowl. See to it that the sweetener dissolves completely.

3. Make the mascarpone cream.

    Use an electric mixer to whip the cream and mascarpone together.

4. Assemble the tiramisu dessert glasses.

    Toss the cake in the coffee-rum mixture so that the cake soaks in the flavors. Don't let the cake stay too long; you don't want it to turn soggy.

    Arrange the tiramisu in the dessert glasses in layers – soaked cake, mascarpone, and grated chocolate. Make another layer.

    Dust the top with cacao powder, if desired.

    Chill the tiramisu for about an hour or more.

CONCLUSION

I'd like to thank you and congratulate you for reading this book from start to finish.

I hope this book was able to deepen your understanding about what a low carb ketogenic diet can do for your health. I hope it has also made you realize that going keto does not mean going without your favorite Italian dishes. You can be healthy and STILL enjoy the amazing food that Italians are well-known for. It is just a matter of replacing the usual high-carb ingredients with keto-friendly ones.

Take inspiration from the recipes provided by the book and impress your family and friends by preparing healthy and mouth-watering appetizers, entrées, and desserts that are at once healthy AND delectable.

The next step is to go to your kitchen and start cooking!

I wish you the best of luck!

Made in the USA
Las Vegas, NV
06 October 2024

96380105R00056